THE VALLEY OF TEARS

A Journey Through Grief

THE VALLEY
OF TEARS

NOLA SHAW

CHRISTIAN ART
PUBLISHERS

Published in South Africa by CHRISTIAN ART PUBLISHERS
PO Box 1599, Vereeniging, 1930

© 2002
First edition 2002

Cover designed by Christian Art Publishers

Unless otherwise indicated, all Scripture quotations are taken
from the *Holy Bible*, New International Version ®. NIV ® Copyright
© 1973, 1978, 1984 by International Bible Society. Used by
permission of Zondervan Publishing House. All rights reserved.
All other Scripture quotations from *THE MESSAGE*.
Copyright © by Eugene H. Peterson 1993, 1994, 1995.
Used by permission of NavPress Publishing Group.

Set in 10 on 12pt Caxton Lt BT by Christian Art Publishers

Printed in China

ISBN 1-86852-925-8

04 05 06 07 08 09 10 11 12 13 – 11 10 9 8 7 6 5 4 3 2

Contents

Foreword

*T*he *Valley of Tears* is written against the background of Nola's deep commitment to Jesus Christ, her sensitive concern for people in pain, careful study and wide experience as a bereavement support group facilitator.

In this booklet Nola offers practical teaching to inform the mind, and gentle encouragement that gives emotional and spiritual direction to the traveler searching for the way through the experience of loss.

She has a masters degree in Theology from UNISA – her dissertation focused on bereavement support.

Rev. Trevor Bosman
Edgemead
Cape Town

CHAPTER 1

God is light

When your loved one died, you probably felt like someone had reached deep within your heart and switched off a light.

This book has been written to reassure you that God's light will never go out. It will shine like a beacon in your darkest hours, guiding you through the turbulent seas of your painful grief to the eternal shoreline of God's love.

There was a time in the Bible when God's people most likely felt the same pain you are feeling in your heart. It was also a time when God's enduring light shone into their dark despair and brought them hope.

The Jewish people had suffered a cruel blow at the hands of their enemies, the Babylonians, who were a powerful, warlike nation. Their king, Nebuchadnezzar, marched on to Jerusalem with his whole army in 587 BC, destroying the holy city of God's people in a brutal attack. The city walls were broken down, the Lord's temple was set on fire, the palace and all the houses and important buildings were razed to the ground. A once vibrant Jerusalem lay in ashes. Thousands lost their lives. Some of the survivors sought refuge in neighboring countries, but a remnant group was deported into exile and scattered in small villages throughout the Babylonian empire. These exiles were forced to live amongst strangers of a different culture who worshiped multiple idols. Many of them became angry, bitter and despondent. Some allowed themselves to become absorbed into the Babylonian way of life, whilst the faithful mourned their homeland and their dead and longed for the day when they would return home.

During this time the anguished people remembered the words of comfort and hope, brought by the Lord's prophet, Isaiah.

Arise, shine, for your light has come,
    and the glory of the Lord rises upon you.

See, darkness covers the earth
    and thick darkness is over the peoples,
but the Lord rises upon you
    and his glory appears over you.

                    ~ Is. 60:1-2 ~

Isaiah proclaimed a message of hope and encouragement, revealing the depth of God's love, understanding and compassion. God's people were suffering an almost unbearable grief, but through the prophet's message they came to realize that God wanted to return them to their promised land, to restore their joy once again. This was their hope, that God would lead them out of a great darkness into His bright light.

I want you to know that God's message of hope and compassion, which Isaiah spoke thousands of years ago, is also intended for you as you walk through your "valley of tears". You may have become angry, bitter and despairing as you struggle in unchartered waters of grief. God the Father sees your tears as you grieve the loss of your beloved. The God who sent His Son to die for the world knows just how you feel, the unbearable sorrow and loss which has splintered your heart into countless fragments. But His light will never go out. Your pain can't keep Him away; it only draws you nearer to Him. If you are a Christian, God is present in your life in a mysterious yet very tangible way. His Holy Spirit, who is also called the Comforter, has come alongside you and will do for you what no-one else can possibly do. He will mend your broken heart.

Though we may endure unbearable sorrow and loss:

God has promised to be with us
The light of God surrounds us
The love of God enfolds us
The power of God protects us
The presence of God is with us
Wherever we are
Wherever our loved one is
GOD IS.

(Adaption of poem by James Dillet Freeman, quoted in *Helping People through Grief* by D. Keuning.)

Chapter 2

Is death the end of life?

Brothers, we do not want you to be igno-
rant about those who fall asleep, or to grieve
like the rest of men, who have no hope. We
believe that Jesus died and rose again and
so we believe that God will bring with Jesus
those who have fallen asleep in him.

~ 1 Thes. 4:13 ~

*J*esus referred to death as falling
asleep more than once. Lazarus had
been dead for four days, and Jesus told
His disciples, *"Our friend Lazarus has fallen
asleep."* He gave the impression that Lazarus, His faithful friend, was quietly resting
and that death was no more threatening
than falling asleep. The story of the raising

of Lazarus from the dead brings a powerful message to faithful Christians. It assures us that Jesus has ultimate power over life and death. Jesus announced that He is " ... *the resurrection and the life. He who believes in me will live, even though he dies; and whoever lives and believes in me will never die*" (Jn. 11:25-26). He conquered death through his cross and resurrection.

Death can be a frightening prospect, but we know that Jesus has gone before us to prepare a place in heaven where all his faithful disciples will join him. *"Do not let your hearts be troubled,"* Jesus says. *"Trust in God, trust also in me. In my Father's house are many rooms; if it were not so, I would have told you. I am going there to prepare a place for you. And if I go and prepare a place for you, I will come back and take you to be with me that you may also be where I am"* (Jn. 14:1-3).

The first Christians also spoke of death as "falling asleep". When addressing the Thessalonian Christians, who were grieving their family and friends persecuted to death for their faith, the apostle Paul used the striking word picture of sleep to describe the state of those who had died. But he did not imply that death is the end of life. Instead, he saw death as a door-way into the eternal realm where God is. When we pass through this door into the world without end, we will take on a spiritual form like that of the resurrected Christ, a transformed body that will live forever with the Lord. Death may be a frightening thought, but the assurance of eternal life ignites hope in our heavy hearts.

We must view the death of fellow Christians as a temporal parting. Christ has promised to return and bring with him every Christian who has "fallen asleep". We can look forward to the great-est reunion of all time, when all believers in Jesus, both dead and alive, will be united in heaven to enjoy fellowship with God forever. Heaven will be the final resting place of every Christian, free from death, sickness, suffering and pain … forever.

D.J. Louw, in *Illness as Crisis and Challenge*, says: "The word heaven refers to a unique space which is determined by God's unique characteristics: love, grace, mercy and charity. Heaven is thus an indication of God's living presence in contrast to our earthly lives."

If your partner is gone, what you had is not over. The love does not stop, only the form of it changes. It is the same in nature; the seasons don't stop happening because one has ended. The cycle goes on. So does your love. Spring doesn't come until winter has fully expressed itself. Give yourself a winter. Mourn your loss. You've known a great love. You still know it. You still have part of it to live. Here is an opportunity to continue to love the one who is gone by sending loving thoughts to him or her, by loving yourself, by smiling at people, by loving others because you know how.

~ Funerals:
Parables for All Occasions, Vol. 2 ~

Note

Numerous Scriptures reveal the marks of true Christians and confirm their final destiny in heaven with Jesus Christ. See for example Jn. 1:12-13; Jn. 3:1-21; Jn. 14:1-4; Jn. 14:21; Rom. 5:1-11; Eph. 2:1-10; 1 Jn. 5:1-5.

CHAPTER 3

Grief: the deepest wound

"My soul is overwhelmed with sorrow to the point of death ... "

~ Mt. 26:38 ~

*T*he Bible gives many examples of people who grieved deeply. Reading about their grief does not lessen our pain, but it surely helps to make us feel human, to understand that grief wounds us all at some time in life.

We are told that David *"fasted ... and spent the nights lying on the ground"* (2 Sam. 12:16) while the son born out of his relationship with Bathsheba lay dying.

Jesus himself experienced intense grief

in the garden of Gethsemane. His disciples lay asleep while he agonized over Judas' treacherous betrayal and his impending death. So deep was his grief that " ... *his sweat was like blood falling to the ground"* (Lk. 22:44).

The Bible also tells us that when Jesus learnt of the execution of John the Baptist, his cousin, he *"withdrew by boat to a solitary place"* (Mt. 14:13) to deal with his grief alone. He removed himself from the hustle and bustle of the crowds which surrounded him daily – he needed space to grieve, just like we all do.

Grief is a common affliction. It is a painful thread which knits all humanity together, for we all experience loss caused by separation at one time or another. The most painful loss, of course, is the death of a loved one.

Doug Manning, in his book *Don't Take My Grief Away*, describes grief as a cut finger.

A cut finger
* is numb before it bleeds
* bleeds before it hurts
* hurts until it begins to heal
* forms a scab and itches until, finally the scab is gone and then a small

scar is left where once there was a wound.

Manning informs us that grief is the deepest wound we will ever experience, and it is like a cut finger which goes through various stages of healing. We need to work through our emotional and physical trauma until we reach the place of acceptance.

Please remember that grief is a process. You must walk through the valley of tears, taking one step at a time. The grief process manifests itself in your emotions, your body, your behavior and even in your spiritual life. The process varies in length from one person to another, depending on personality, relationships and circumstances. Each person is different; we all express grief in different ways. One person may come to terms with his grief within four months of his loss while another may only begin to cope after eighteen months of bereavement. Others may take two years or more. What matters most is that we are working through our grief rather than supressing it.

S.R. Sullender, in his book *Grief and Growth*, says that grief is painful and seldom welcomed but it is necessary. It is hard work and it is good, because its purpose is to restore the bereaved to wholeness again. Grief is not your enemy, but a friend.

C.S. Lewis, who lost his wife to cancer, wrote the following words about grief in his personal diary:

> "I thought I could describe a state; make a map of sorrow. Sorrow, however, turns out to be not a state but a process. It needs not a map but a history … There is something new to be chronicled every day. Grief is like a long valley, a winding valley where any bend may reveal a totally new landscape."

Remember, your grief is normal. It is a natural gift from God so your hurt may heal.

Chapter 4

Why?

God, God ... my God. Why did you dump
me miles from nowhere? Doubled up with
pain, I call to God all the day long. No
answer. Nothing. I keep at it all night,
tossing and turning. And you! Are you
indifferent, above it all ... ?

~ Ps. 22 (The Message) ~

*E*ugene Peterson's contemporary ar-
rangement of Psalm 22 paints a
profound word picture of what the psalmist was feeling during a time of trial and
suffering. He was questioning God, who
he believed had deserted him, leaving him
to his own devices. He was desolate and
in despair.

When Jesus cried out in agony from
the Cross of Calvary, he spoke the same

desperate words the psalmist had written centuries before: *"My God, my God, why have you abandoned me?"*

When calamity strikes us, we may feel the same loneliness. Our natural response is to look for answers to the interminable question "Why?" Why is this happening to me? Why did he die so young? We prayed for healing – why did you take her away from us? Why …?

You want answers, but receive none. In the confusion of questions welling up within your heart you seek to find a home for blame and mistakenly place it on others. Ultimately, you may feel that somehow God is to blame for your pain. You may even doubt that He exists!

Men and women of faith throughout the ages have been pierced by pangs of doubt, questioning God's will for their lives. You may feel out of control, but you are not alone.

Philip Yancey says:

"Jesus gave no philosophical answer to the problem of pain, but He did give an existential answer. I cannot learn from Him why bad things occur, but I can learn how God feels about it. I look at how Jesus responds to the sisters of his good friend

Lazarus, or to a leprosy patient banned from the town gates. Jesus gives God a face, and that face is streaked with tears."

CHAPTER 5

I can't accept this!

The moon will shine like the sun, and the
sunlight will be seven times brighter, like
the light of seven full days, when the Lord
binds up the bruises of his people and heals
the wounds …

~ Is. 30:26 ~

A scripture verse like this is intended to encourage us, but if you are struggling to accept that your loved one is gone, brighter days will be hidden behind a gloomy fog bank. You may feel like this at the moment, trapped in an unreal state. Every time the phone rings, you hope to hear the voice of your beloved. Or perhaps you feel like you will awake from a bad dream and discover that your loved one is only away on holiday.

Have you been trying to protect yourself from the pain by denying the facts? Have you been holding on to your loved one's possessions, retaining a room exactly as it was before the death, or even blocking out the memory of circumstances surrounding the death?

This is called denial – a normal outworking of grief, especially in the early stages. It may take you many months of working through your grief before you can finally accept death as a natural part of being human. It may be a long, winding road before you are finally able to close this chapter of your life and accept that you will never see your loved one again on earth. But take heart. God himself will restore your relationship in heaven one day in a way more beautiful than you can ever imagine.

CHAPTER 6

I feel so stressed

In my distress I called to the Lord; I cried to my God for help. He reached down from on high and took hold of me; he drew me out of deep waters. He rescued me from my powerful enemy, from my foes, who were too strong for me. They confronted me in the day of my disaster, but the Lord was my support. He brought me out into a spacious place; he rescued me because he delighted in me.

~ Ps. 18:6,16-19 ~

David must have written this psalm when he was under great stress. We see evidence of this early in the psalm when he says anxiously, " ... *the cords of death entangled me; the torrents of destruction overwhelmed me*" (18:4).

This psalm is essentially a prayer of thanksgiving to God for His support and protection of David during his battles against Saul and his other enemies, when he felt helpless and defenseless. David instinctively knew that God was his refuge and healer, and this deep faith helped him stand under the weight of his problems which threatened to overpower him.

God also knows your stress as you battle with your grief. Facing an unknown future without your loved one may leave you feeling defenseless, weak, helpless and unprepared for the new challenges life will bring across your path. The sudden changes which death brings in its wake can cause unbearable tension and stress, which in turn can affect your physical, mental and behavioral well-being. You may find yourself complaining about headaches, a heavy chest, digestive changes such as overeating or appetite loss, breathlessness, muscle contractions, raised blood pressure, restlessness, a sense of unreality and an aching yearning.

Don't let these symptoms alarm you. They are a normal part of the grief process. In time, manifestations like these will ease. For extra peace of mind, consult your personal physician for a physical check-up.

If your tensions and stress become un-bearable, allow God to 'rescue' you from your helplessness. Be still before Him and permit Him to take hold of you while you walk through the valley of tears. In His time He will bring you healing.

CHAPTER 7

I feel so guilty

———

Count yourself lucky, how happy you must be – you get a fresh start, your slate's wiped clean. Count yourself lucky – God holds nothing against you and you're holding nothing back from him. When I kept it all inside, my bones turned to powder, my words became daylong groans. The pressure never let up; all the juices of my life dried up. Then I let it all out; I said, "I'll make a clean breast of my failures to God." Suddenly the pressure was gone – my guilt dissolved, my sin disappeared.

~ Ps. 32 (THE MESSAGE) ~

Grief often gives rise to emotions of guilt and self-reproach, which force us to question our own conduct. We embark on vigorous soul searching, asking questions of ourselves about our behavior towards the deceased prior to their death: Did I show enough patience when my loved one could no longer help himself? Should I have looked for a second opinion? Did I do enough for him? Why didn't I tell him how much I loved him? Why didn't I thank him for the good times? Did I do everything to prevent this death? Could I have done anything else? Why did I leave the argument unresolved?

In the early stages of grief, questioning ourselves is a normal part of grief. Genuine guilt must be confronted and dealt with or it will become suppressed, resulting in deep depression which will eventually need to be clinically treated.

In his penitential Psalm 32, David is stricken with guilt because of his wrong doing. He confesses his guilt to God and experiences a flood of forgiveness which washes away his sin.

If you are feeling genuine guilt and self-reproach about unresolved matters between yourself and your loved one, don't be too hard on yourself. Firstly, you need to learn to forgive yourself and think of the many positive things you did for your loved one. You will most likely discover that they outweigh the negatives.

The Bible encourages us to bring our

guilty feelings to the Lord. Remember, Jesus is your intercessor. Confess your shortcomings to Him and ask for forgiveness. It is a free gift. This is the key to complete freedom from guilt and self-reproach.

CHAPTER 8

I'm so angry

───────※※───────

Answer me when I call you, O my righteous
God. Give me release from my distress; be
merciful and hear my prayer.

~ Ps. 4:1 ~

*I*n Psalm 4 the psalmist calls out to
the Lord in a time of great distress
and calamity. We don't really know what
his problems were, but his impatience,
anger and frustration are obvious from
the tone of his words: *"Answer me when I
call you."*

Perhaps like the psalmist you are feeling frustrated and angry as grief takes
its toll in your life. Anger is a normal
reaction to grief following the death of a
loved one, but it must be managed and
pointed in the right direction. If it is not

harnessed, it may lead to hasty decisions and actions that will be deeply regretted at a later stage. Coupled with this, misdirected anger can also be internalized, resulting in severe depression which will eventually need professional treatment.

Philip Yancey, in *Reaching For The Invisible God*, told the story of Don Wonderhope who was the father of an eleven-year-old girl who contracted leukemia. Just as the bone marrow began to respond to treatment and she approached remission, an infection swept through the ward and killed her. Wonderhope, who had brought in a cake with his daughter's name on it, left the hospital, returned to the church where he had prayed for her healing, and hurled the cake at the crucifix hanging in front of the church. The cake hit just beneath the crown of thorns and brightly colored icing dripped down Jesus' face of stone.

Misdirected anger? God was the target of that man's anger. How can a loving God allow such a thing to happen? If God is supposed to be loving, he had lost all respect for Him. His anger alienated him from God and probably left him racked with guilt.

Sometimes we are not only angry with

God. We turn on the attending physician, anesthetist, insensitive nursing care in the hospital, uncaring relatives, friends and even ourselves.

Verbalize your anger. Who are you angry at? The one who has died? Some-one else? You can be totally honest with God. Tell Him how angry you feel. Pour your angry emotions out before Him. He understands all that you are going through. His love for you is unchanged by your anger. Trust Him to help you deal with your emotions – be assured that He listens to your prayers. You cannot change what has happened, but God promises to work *"for the good of those who love him"* (Rom. 8:28). He will answer in the best possible way for your healing and well-being.

CHAPTER 9

I feel so fearful

But now this is what the Lord says – he who created you, O Jacob, he who formed you O Israel; "Fear not, for I have redeemed you; I have summoned you by name; you are mine. When you pass through the waters, I will be with you; and when you pass through the rivers, they will not sweep over you. When you walk through fire, you will not be burned; The flames will not set you ablaze. For I am the LORD, your God, the Holy one of Israel, your Savior."

~ Is. 43:1-3 ~

God's people were torn from their homeland and driven into exile for many years. They experienced a torturous grief. Then Isaiah the prophet brought them a powerful message of comfort and protection. They felt anxious about returning to the land God had given them, but Isaiah's message was intended to calm their fears.

What are you fearful of? Is it a future of loneliness and uncertainty? One of the manifestations of grief is fear.

If you stand on the wall of one of South Africa's big dams when the sluice gates are opened you will witness a terrifying yet awesome sight as millions of liters of water pour forcefully out, churning and swirling into the river below. Everything is swept up in the raging torrent – no living being could possibly survive the fury of the water.

There are other wonders of nature equally terrifying. Summer in the Western Cape brings with it the ominous danger of mountain fires that sweep over huge tracts of land, destroying flora and fauna in its path. Nothing can withstand the heat of the flames, especially when fanned by gale force winds. The destructive power of flames raging out of control is no less awesome than the strength of unleashed water.

Grief has the same rampant power as fire and water; scorching our hearts and churning our emotions into a whirlpool of despair. Like God's ancient people, everything familiar and loved can be swept away in a moment with the force of rushing water or the destruction of burning flames.

If you feel as if you are being swept along by the raging torrent of grief, remember that experiencing fear is part of the healing process. If God can calm the waters and direct the fires, how much more will He strengthen and deliver you from fear? Even though you must pass through the waters of grief, God promises that you will not be drowned if you trust Him. Neither will the fire burn you if you allow Him to be your guide.

Take strength from these words:

The LORD is my light and my salvation –
  whom shall I fear?
The LORD is the stronghold of my life –
  of whom shall I be afraid?

~ Ps. 27:1 ~

CHAPTER 10

I feel so alone

The LORD is my Shepherd I shall not be in want. He makes me lie down in green pastures, he leads me beside quiet waters, he restores my soul. He guides me in paths of righteousness for his name's sake. Even though I walk through the valley of the shadow of death I will fear no evil, for you are with me; your rod and your staff, they comfort me. You prepare a table before me in the presence of my enemies, you anoint my head with oil; my cup overflows. Surely goodness and love will follow me all the days of my life, and I will dwell in the house of the LORD forever.

~ Ps. 23 ~

Sheep are notoriously defenseless animals, often falling prey to predators or wandering astray. The shepherd performs a vital function in the life of his sheep, tenderly and caringly watching over his flock. When they are lost and alone he searches for them, bringing them home before darkness falls. He binds their injuries, waters and feeds them, and gives them a safe place to sleep.

Our Heavenly Father loves you with the tenderness of a shepherd who watches over his flock day and night. When life threatens to overwhelm you in dark clouds of loneliness, know that God is near you. It may feel as if He is a million miles away, but He is with you in the bad times as much as in the good times. God is a refuge for the vulnerable, lonely and defenseless.

King David, the author of the well-known Psalm 23, solemnly affirms God's precious love for you. God promises to restore you, to strengthen you and accompany you as you work through your grief.

CHAPTER 11

I'm so weary

Do you not know? Have you not heard? The Lord is the everlasting God, the Creator of the ends of the earth. He will not grow weary, and his understanding no one can fathom. He gives strength to the weary and increases the power of the weak. Even youths grow tired and weary, and young men stumble and fall; but those who hope in the Lord will renew their strength. They will soar on wings like eagles; they will run and not grow weary, they will walk and not be faint.

~ Is. 40:28-31 ~

In Greek mythology, Sisyphus' fate was to push a great stone up a mountain, only to have it roll down again before reaching the top. This feeling that the job is endless, that you can never quite reach the top of the mountain, no matter how hard you try, can lead to exhaustion.

In the same way, grief can lead to weariness, near exhaustion and despondency. Just when you think you are beginning to cope with your emotions, you slide back down the mountain slope into the mists of painful longing and loneliness.

Has your loss made you a stranger to yourself? Is weariness of body, mind and heart taking over your daily life? If the things you used to enjoy – a walk on the beach, a day's shopping, dining at your favorite restaurant, watching your favorite TV program, having friends and family around – no longer occupy your attention for very long, then your grief is probably wearing you out.

Eagles often build their nests high up on the face of steep precipices. The female lays her eggs in a carefully constructed nest and after the eaglets have hatched, she nurtures and cares for them until they grow stronger. As the eaglets grow older the space in their nest grows smaller, and sometimes the weakest one, weary from fighting its more robust siblings, gets pushed out of the nest. The ever-attentive mother eagle swoops down on the eaglet plunging hundreds of meters to a certain death, gathering it up safely in her outstretched wings.

God does the same for you when you are weary and grief is threatening to pull you off the side of the mountain into a painful abyss. Like the mother eagle, He rescues you and gives you strength to soar. Call on Him in faith and expectancy and know that in His own wonderful way, He is flying with you in your struggles to cope with your unfamiliar and frightening emotions.

CHAPTER 12

I have no peace

Rejoice in the Lord always. I will say it again: Rejoice! Let your gentleness be evident to all. The Lord is near. Do not be anxious about anything, but in everything by prayer and petition, with thanksgiving, present your requests to God, and the peace of God which transcends all understanding will guard your hearts and minds in Christ Jesus.

~ Phil. 4:4-7 ~

The apostle Paul encouraged Christians living in Philippi to turn their anxieties, which are robbers of peace, into prayers. They would then experience peace, he assured them, not a peace which the world knows but a peace which is the result of the Holy Spirit of God at work in their lives.

Jesus promised peace to His disciples. Their security lay with Him. In the same way, Jesus wants to restore you to wholeness and peace, a life of new hope for the future. Remember, God experienced loss and pain when His Son died on the cross, so He can empathize with you like no one else in this world.

Right now your greatest need is to experience quietness and rest in your spirit and healing from your grief. God's Holy Spirit is able to do that for you. It is only through His power that you can and will experience a deep, peaceful quieting of your riotous emotions. In the final chapter you will read of some practical steps you can take to facilitate this quietness and rest.

CHAPTER 13

Healing tears

You've kept track of my every toss and turn through the sleepless nights, each tear entered in your ledger, each ache written in your book.

~ Ps. 56 (THE MESSAGE) ~

J. S. Worden, in *Grief Counseling and Grief Therapy: A Handbook for the Mental Health Practitioner*, speaks about research which has been undertaken into the function of tears:

"There has been interesting speculation that tears may have potential healing value. Stress causes chemical imbalance in the body, and some researchers believe that tears remove toxic substances and help re-establish homeostasis. They hypothesize that the chemical content of tears caused by emotional stress is different from that of tears secreted as a function of eye irritation. Tests are being done to see what type of mood-altering chemicals produced by the brain are present in emotional tears. Tears do relieve emotional stress, but how they do this is still a question. Further research is needed on the deleterious effects, if any, of suppressed crying."

In Psalm 56 we read that King David came to the realization that God knew his profound sorrows and he was equally certain that God understood his grief. Even better still, God acknowledged his tears.

There is no doubt that tears are one of God's greatest healing gifts to a broken heart. Tears are a normal reaction to grief and should not be seen as a sign of weakness. Each shed tear is one more small step toward healing and restoration.

Society erroneously calls for the "stiff upper lip". But by denying your grieving tears you are suppressing your deepest emotions – this can lead to deep-seated emotional problems which will probably surface later in life.

Remember, just because you are a

Christian does not mean you may not cry. Jesus wept. If we have a relationship with God through Jesus, no tear rolls down our cheek without our Father in heaven taking notice.

N.T. Wright, in *Following Jesus*, has captured the essence of God's care for His grieving people in a poignant poem:

> After the tears comes the silence;
> the slow night, the still sad time,
> rinsed, empty, scoured and sore with salt,
> spent waiting without hope.
> After the night comes the Lamb
> bright morning star, with living water free
> and fresh, the fruit of Friday's toil.

CHAPTER 14

Moving on

You did it: you changed wild lament into
whirling dance; You ripped off my black
mourning band and decked me with
wildflowers. I'm about to burst with song;
I can't keep quiet about you. God, my
God, I can't thank you enough.

~ Ps. 30 (THE MESSAGE) ~

*E*ugene Peterson's modern translation
of David's jubilant prayer of thanksgiving is outstanding. Can you sense
David's giddy joy breaking out like the
dawn of a new day? God wants you to
have the same joy as David when he was
delivered from his "wild lament". He wants
to heal the wounds and bruises of your
grief.

You may ask, "When will this pain go

away? Will I ever stop grieving?"

S.R. Sullender, in *Grief and Growth*, says:

> "Many people have likened grief to a journey through a long dark tunnel. The darkness of the tunnel is grief's pain and anguish. The light at the end of the tunnel is their new life. The only way out is through. In time, the light at the end of the tunnel grows larger and larger, the darkness of pain recedes ever so gradually. Finally, there comes a stage when we can say, 'I think I am through it.'"

The intense period of grieving is over when you can:

- ❊ remember your loved one without experiencing searing pain
- ❊ accept both negatives and positives of your loss
- ❊ cope successfully with new skills taken over from the lost loved one
- ❊ withdraw intense emotional energy from your beloved and reinvest in other occupations or relationships
- ❊ realize that the special relationship you had can never be replaced, and that the memory must remain in your heart, thus freeing you to move on.

CHAPTER 15

What can I do to help myself cope?

Grief is something we cannot deny or escape, as much as we may like to. The only way to deal with your pain is to work through it, one day at a time. You are the only person who can do it – no one else can do it for you.

The following are a few practical hints to help you cope:

※ Allow yourself time to grieve.
※ Call upon the Lord in prayer, asking for His comfort, strength and compassion.
※ Read your Bible, especially the Psalms, daily or as often as you need encouragement.
※ Write a letter to your loved one saying

all the things you wish you had said before his death – write the positives and negatives.

- ❊ Keep a journal of your day to day physical pains, emotions and behavior.
- ❊ Don't hold back your tears.
- ❊ Don't let others dissuade you from doing what is right for you.
- ❊ Forgive those you are angry at.
- ❊ Play soothing music, especially the kind which focuses your thoughts on the Lord.
- ❊ Don't shut yourself off completely from others.
- ❊ Find someone who is genuinely interested in your well-being and talk about your pain.
- ❊ Eat nourishing food.
- ❊ Don't rely on alcohol or prescription drugs to get you through.
- ❊ Don't block painful memories – work through them.
- ❊ Don't make hasty decisions about your lifestyle, such as selling your home, moving in with relatives or to another town; rather give yourself time to work through some of the pain.
- ❊ Find someone reputable to assist you with your financial affairs.
- ❊ Join a bereavement support group,

where you can share your pain with others who are going through grief as well.

- ❈ Ask for assistance if you need it – your minister and church members will be only too pleased to help you.
- ❈ Grief is a process to be worked through. Set your own pace. Some people take longer than others to work through their pain.
- ❈ Don't be impatient if your progress is slow.
- ❈ View a beautiful sunset and meditate on the wonder of God.
- ❈ Live one day at a time.

Prayer

Gentle Jesus, Comforter of the sorrowing –
comfort me.
Healer of painful wounds, heal me.
Let me feel Your sacred presence.
Strengthen and empower me.
Wash away all fear and dread.
Come, O come, walk with me.

"Come to me all you who are weary and burdened and I will give you rest. Take my yoke upon you and learn from me for I am gentle and humble in heart, and you will find rest for your souls. For my yoke is easy and my burden is light."

~ Mt. 11:28-30 ~